U CAN SURVIVE AND THRIVE

Sink or Swim

Fight or Flight

They Both Chose To FIGHT

Written By: LaToya T. Jackson &
Susie Walker-Byrd

Table of Contents

"For I know the plans I have for you," declares the LORD. Plans to prosper you and not to harm you, plans to give you a hope and a future."

Jeremiah 29:11

	ACKNOWLEDGEMENTS	i
CHAPTER 1:	SURVIVE	1
CHAPTER 2:	SUBMISSION	19
CHAPTER 3:	UNIQUENESS	27
CHAPTER 4:	RESTORATION	36
CHAPTER 5:	VESSEL	43
CHAPTER 6:	IMAGINE	50
CHAPTER 7:	VICTORY	56
CHAPTER 8:	EXPECTANCY	62
CHAPTER 9:	AFTER THE STORM	67
	STAYING CONNECTED	75

ACKNOWLEDGEMENTS

LaToya

To my Heavenly Father, you and you alone know all the tears I've shed, the sleepless nights I've endured and the relentless pain I feel in my heart, but you've kept me through it all. I TRUST your will for my life God is bigger than my pain; use me!

To Jarrod Allen Jackson, you are the wind beneath my wings. You taught me true, uncontainable love. From working 40 hours during the week, then traveling six hours on Friday evenings after work (from Cleveland, OH to Bardstown, KY), to working at my boutique and at various festivals the entire weekend, selling women's clothes. To only turnaround late Sunday evening and begin the same six hour pilgrimage back home to Cleveland, to be at work on Monday morning, because of the unconditional love and support you had for me. You repeated the same grueling cycle for months, without complaint. You taught me to laugh more, to be less uptight, and to live and let live. It's been hard going on without you. I've made it my mission to honor your legacy and to work hard to make you proud; by living a purpose driven life. I feel your presence and I know without a shadow of a doubt that you LIVE. Your death will never ever be in vain. As long as I live baby, you live!

To my sister LaTasha Calbert, if I had 10,000 tongues it wouldn't be enough. You were there by my side through it all. You left your child, uprooted your life for 6 months, to move to Cleveland to be with me, that's love girl. I love you sissy, more than I could ever express.

Angela Calbert, my listening ear, the one who stays up with me until the sun comes up and never complains. To the one, who took on another child (our nephew) for the 6 months Tasha stayed with me in Cleveland. Thank you, sissy. I adore you more than you will ever know.

To Demitra Newby, I thank you for the love and camaraderie that we shared while both grieving the loss of Jaylin and Jarrod. Thank you, Newby, and Snook for welcoming me into your home. The late night talks, ice cream binge sessions and catching up on our TV shows was time I will forever cherish. No matter the distance, I love you.

To my parents, I know it's been hard for you both seeing your once vibrant, ambitious and ready to rule the world daughter; completely defeated, depleted, and ready to die. I know it's been hard and you've supported me the best way you both know how.

Momma, thank you for the word's that still give me strength to this day. When I said I couldn't go on, and that I didn't want to plan Jarrod's funeral, you told me I had to. "No one would put the love and detail into making it perfect for, him, baby the way you would". Thank you for praying over me in the funeral home, covering me. It was your love and words of wisdom that gave me the extra steam I needed to push pass my own pain and look at the bigger picture. I love you, momma, more than I could ever express in words. I've always attempted to go above and beyond for you, so that my actions would reflect my respect and admiration, without my words having to.

Daddy, you are one of my best friends and I thank you. I know that I always have you. From teaching me how to ride a bike, forcing me to sit at the kitchen table to perfect my math problems, to picking me up at the front of

Jarrod's casket; you've always been there for me and I can't imagine my life without a father like you.

To my niece and nephew Isaiah and Azariah, who knew the presence of such sweet, little, souls could be so POWERFUL in the midst of such catastrophe?

Isaiah your drawings and cards of Uncle Jarrod and I brought me happy tears.

Zari you have the kindest, most loving and gentle spirit, your hugs and protective spirit sooth my broken heart more than you will ever know.

I love you babies as if you were mine. Your warm hugs, kisses and tears for the hurt you witnessed your Auntie Toy endure will never be forgotten. Thank you forever and ever for your unconditional love for me and Uncle Jarrod. He is proud of the way you have cared for me.

Anthony Beckham, you are the definition of a best friend. I know that Jarrod is so grateful you've kept an eye out for his wife. You are one of the few people from my life with Jarrod that continue to stay connected to me. I can't tell you how much that means to me. I love you like a brother and that will never, ever change.

Breanna Cobbs-Bacon, when I say I love you I sincerely mean it. Friends like you are few, and far in between. From getting me out of the house, to calling and texting to check on me, to encouraging me to pursue my dreams; you've always remained present, even when I was distant. Thank you for not turning your back on me, when so many others have. I don't take our friendship lightly.

Mickel Green, my younger, big brother. Thank you for constantly checking on me and making your presence felt in my life. The dream you had shortly after Jarrod transitioned, gave me peace and reassurance at a very uncertain time in my life. I'm not surprised that you were one of the first that he chose to come to. I love you.

To my girlfriends, boyfriends, Facebook friends, and strangers all across the world, I know that it is without a doubt that your relentless prayers, without ceasing, is why I am still here. Thank you ALL for standing in the gap for me. My prayer is that God blesses you all tenfold, for everything that you've poured into me. Please continue to keep me lifted. It's still very, very hard and I will continue to pray for you all, as well.

Last but certainly not least, it is without an ounce of doubt, that the connection between me and Susie Walker-Byrd was divinely orchestrated and executed by our Lord and Savior Jesus Christ. At the last minute, the table seating was "mysteriously" changed and for unknown reasons we were seated together at the Emmaus Walk Christian Retreat. This allowed us to bond spiritually and relationally. Thank you for being a friend to me at the darkest hour of my life. Your sisterhood, partnership and kind, nurturing spirit has been a blessing to me. My prayer is that we both use our stories to bless and encourage the lives of the masses while also searching for hope, healing and restoration.

I love you all!

Susie

Co-writing this book would not be possible without the leading of the Holy Spirit and the obedience of my dear friend, LaToya Jackson. Thank you, Lord, for bringing me through the treatments of cancer with a positive mindset. You've allowed me to finish strong and have a desire to encourage others in this unsolicited battle. Thank you for allowing LaToya and I to cross paths on a spiritual retreat and become close sisters in Christ. (The Emmaus Walk #143, Table of Deborah)

To my mother, the late Pauline Gaddie, though you are with the Lord your presence lives forever in my heart. I am the woman I am today because of you. I am grateful for your "giving" spirit. I keep your heart beating through my passion to help and give hope to others. I love you mama and I'll see you in Heaven when my journey is complete.

To all cancer warriors, receiving a cancer diagnosis can be overwhelming especially when your support system is limited to none. My hope is to be a source of inspiration, a resource, and support along the journey.

You do not have to do this alone!

To my husband, Shelby Byrd Sr., your unwavering faith is reassuring. Thank you for your love, prayers, and continuous support that nurtured me back to health. You are my rock and **I love you**!

To a few of my closest friends; Malisa Wiley, Robin McAdams, Calquetta Williams and Brande Sherrer; thank you for your friendship and listening ear. Your faith, encouragement, and laughter meant so much. My sweet friend Dana Canedy, thank you for making sure I had the best *"me-time"* ever! Thank you Peacola Beauchamp for sitting with me through chemo treatment.

To my God-sister, Fay Harris and family, thank you for your loving support and taking care of my children, which allowed me to focus on my health and recovery. Specifically, to my niece Taylor, thank you for your prayers and keeping your cousins encouraged during this scary time. To my daughters, Brooke and Bria, thank you for showing strength, being brave, and doing your best in school, you make me so proud.

To my son, Bryce Walker-Byrd, thank you for reminding me that we are warriors, we never give up. Your love and strength pushed me through those dreadful chemo treatments.

To my pastors, Edward and Nicole Griffith, and *The Way Christian Church* family, I was truly blessed with your fervent prayers. Thank you all for your genuine love and support.

To my God-mother, Rev. Herlea Reynolds, who God used to stand in the gap as my mother. Mother Reynolds provided me with continuous love, prayer, encouragement and support. Thank you to my mentor Rachael Miller for your prayers and encouragement to move into my God-given destiny.

Richard Barbour my amazing big brother, your encouragement is calming. Thank you for loving your baby sister and keeping me close. To my awesome sister-in-law Sharmene Barbour, your support and wisdom is a valuable addition to my life, I love you! To my sister Linda, thank you for supporting my food cravings. To my niece, Cynthia Rollins, your support and faith meant so much, thank you!

To the *Jill's Wish Foundation*, I'm so grateful for your vision to help other warriors. I'm honored and appreciative for the partnership and synergy created with Susie's Strength.

Special thanks to my doctors and their staff; Myra Henderson, Adam Lye, Allison Hatmaker and Dean Tindall.

Last but not least, a big thank you to my JCPS Buechel Alternative School family for your encouragement; Joey Riddle, Rita Succession and Theresa Whitlow I appreciate you.

CHAPTER 1

LaToya Jackson and **Susie Walker-Byrd,** met while attending a three day Spiritual Retreat. Over that weekend the ladies bonded, because of life altering events that had taken place in their lives. They learned 2014 was a very traumatic year for the both of them. Right before Christmas, while others were enjoying Yuletide blessings with family and friends, both ladies received news that would change their lives, FOREVER!

After 33 long years, LaToya had finally tied the knot and was excited to share her life with her best friend and new husband. Unfortunately, two months after their magical wedding day, her husband Jarrod died unexpectedly at the age of 31, due to a rare disease that she was unaware he had.

In the blink of an eye, Susie went from being a busy wife, mother, and practicing Social Worker; to a woman literally fighting for her life. Susie was diagnosed with stage 1 Triple Negative Breast Cancer, the most deadly type of breast cancer that one can have.

Although the ladies had no incline of the other's existence, the two had come to an impasse simultaneously.

FIGHTING two very different, but equally earthshattering battles. It was either SINK or SWIM, FIGHT or FLIGHT.

They both chose to **FIGHT**!

LaToya's Story

Months and months of disrespect, degradation and discrimination had all come to a head. I found myself in a stall, in the women's bathroom at my job, crying my eyes out, pleading with my new husband, Jarrod, that I couldn't take anymore.

For over a year, I and another black manager endured racial innuendos, retaliatory and subpar treatment in addition to bullying from our superiors. When we attempted to escalate the issues, we were disingenuously placated with false claims to mitigate and rectify our complaints, however, nothing ever changed.

For an entire year, I worked in an utterly hostile and uncomfortable environment with people that I knew didn't want me there. However, I had recently closed the doors on my own clothing business, relocating to Cleveland, OH to finally be with my man.

A New Beginning

June 9th, 2013 we were in Buffalo, NY. The day prior we had attended one of Jarrod's high school teammate's wedding. We decided to visit Niagara Falls while we were there.

It was an absolutely magical day. We got up early and headed to see the falls. We walked around window shopping, before deciding on a tour. From there we were chauffeured to different attractions along the falls. We stood in amazement, marvelling at what God created.

The day was PERFECT, the weather was PERFECT and the man by my side was PERFECT. We were almost done with our trip. We were taken to the last destination on the tour, which was the best destination. We were right in the vortex, the nucleus of the falls, as high as we could get. I was on cloud 9, in pure bliss, while gazing at the rushing water I began to dance in place. I just felt so incredibly blessed to be in such a beautiful place with the person I loved the most.

Jarrod called my name, it was as if I had been dreaming while awake, because it took him a few tries before he fully got my attention. As I turned to look at him, he began saying "I just love you so much baby, I just love you" as he began to go down on one knee, with the rock I had been praying for. I was in awe. I couldn't speak. For what seems like minutes, I stared at him in pure and utter disbelief.

"Will you be my wife?" I responded with tears, belting out an emotional YES, YES, YES!!!! We hugged, cried and basked in the newness of being newly engaged, while onlookers and tourists cheered us on.

That was one of the top 3 BEST days of my life. Thinking back on that day fills my heart with uncontainable joy.

After the newness of being engaged set in, it was time to plan a wedding. But, in order to pay for it, I needed a job. Thankfully, after a few months, I found a job that paid decent, but came with a lot of baggage that I didn't sign up for. However, my goal was to stay long enough to help pay for my wedding and build a sizable nest egg, before finding something else. Plus, I needed the insurance and the vacation time.

For over a year, I got up every day and forced myself to go into a place that I was not wanted or valued, but I endured for the goal. (The goal of building with my life partner, the issues I experienced were temporary, that's what I told myself.) No pain, no gain....right?!

I did exactly what I set out to do. I stayed long enough for us to afford the wedding of our dreams. I stayed long enough for us to save half of our goal. However, everything came to a head one day in November, when I called my husband and told him, this is it "I can't do it anymore, I'm walking out."

Although two incomes are always better than one, he reassured me we would be okay. I had the blessing of my new husband, to disconnect from a place that had been the biggest source of my stress and frustrations for 1 ½ years.

As I left the building, I instantly felt a load lifted from my shoulders. I had a man that loved me, supported me and had my back. We were in this thing called life, together.

December 17, 2014

My husband was coming home late, his company was taking them somewhere different every day for the holiday season. He and I had talked throughout the day via Facebook messenger. Our conversations were the funniest. He called me on his way to his last destination, talking about one of his co-workers and how bad his breath was. We laughed, exchanged I love you's and that was it.

That was the last time I would ever hear his laugh, his voice, his sarcasm.

Just two months after our dream wedding, 1 ½ years after working a job that I hated, after closing my business and moving to start my life with this man that I loved more than life, it was ALL over, just like that. He was gone at the age of 31, from a massive heart attack while driving home.

Life as I knew it was over. My hopes, dreams, and aspirations all came to a screeching halt on that cold winter night in December.

How Do I Live Without You?

I became a hollow shell. I felt empty and alone. Many people were around me, talking to me, hugging me attempting to encourage me, but they were talking to a mannequin, a clone of some sort that resembled me, but was not me or the person formally known as me. Jarrod's soul had left his earthly shell, but my heart died right along with him, when I received the news that the man I chose to spend the rest of my days with, the man I chose to build a family and an empire with, the man that just 2 months prior took my hand in marriage and asked me to be his FOREVER, was gone.

Celine Dion's song "How Do I Live Without You", became the theme song of my life.

> How do I live without you? I want to know.
>
> How do I breathe without you? If you ever go.
>
> How do I ever, ever SURVIVE?
>
> How do I, how do I, Oh how do I live?

How do you rebound from something as final as death? There is no resurrecting the one you love. Once our number has been called, that's it, our time is up.

As a Christian, I struggled with accepting the fact that my husband was taken from me. It was incredibly hard to wrap my mind around the fact that a loving God would allow this to happen.

December 23, 2014

Susie's Story

Unlike every other day, I'm usually rushing to get to my destination, especially this time of the year. Christmas was fast approaching, only two days away. Everyone was finishing their last minute shopping, but on this particular day, everything was slow motion for me. I was in no hurry to get to my doctor's appointment, in fact, I took my sweet time as I rode in silence. No radio, no cell phone, just complete silence, while thinking about what news my doctor would deliver to me. I knew it wasn't good news, because the call I received to come into the office, was different from the others. The office manager called, instead of the front desk clerk who normally called. Her tone was gentle and filled with compassion. I sensed that she wanted so badly to say "I'm so sorry". However, she began to say "Mrs. Byrd we got the results back from your biopsy and Dr. Henderson would like for you to come in to discuss the results of your test". That was the first red flag for me, because normally if everything is ok they don't call. Like the old cliché, "no news is good news." I was concerned, but not fearful. Years prior, I had a cancer scare that turned out to be nothing. Thinking about all of the possible outcomes, I tried to convince myself that this time was probably the same as the one before. Nonetheless, I knew I had to go in and I chose to go alone. I wanted to process whatever my doctor was going to say, before discussing it with anyone.

After checking in, I sat patiently in the waiting room, looking at various individuals and wondering what news they were getting. Most of the women were pregnant, as I was at an O.B. doctor's office. Some of the women looked happy and excited, with their mate beside them. Others looked not so happy, they actually appeared miserable, as if they were ready to deliver at any moment. Either way, they were all there for a momentous occasion, babies are such a blessing. As I sat there allowing my mind to run wild, I remember thinking "even though pregnancy didn't agree with me, I'd rather be pregnant and in any of their shoes, than what I was there for".

They finally called my name. As I stood, slowly walking back to the exam room, for the first time since receiving the call, I actually felt fear. I instantly felt in my gut, that my life was about to change forever.

When my usually upbeat doctor walked into the room, not so upbeat; with a look on her face that I had never seen, worry, fear, anxiety and uncertainty swept through my body. She sat down, (which is something she has never done) and didn't say her usual tagline "Life is good". I immediately asked her hesitantly, "Is life not good?" She gave a gentle smile and responded "yes, life is good". Even though she said it, I wasn't convinced. I instantly knew then, that my life involved cancer. She took a second to gain her composure, sighed and confirmed what I already knew "it's cancer".

Everything stopped, I sat there in a daze looking at her as though she was speaking a foreign language. A barrage of questions filled my mind, all I could think was "What am I supposed to do with this? What do I do now? How do I get this out of my body?" My mind was in overdrive, while my exterior appeared numb and lifeless. For one of the first times in my life, I was speechless. The room went completely silent, for what seemed like forever. I looked at her waiting for instructions on how to move forward.

With a sense of urgency, Dr. Henderson proceeded to recommend a good surgeon, one she would go to if she were in my position. That was somewhat comforting to know that she was sending me to "the best".

Shortly thereafter, I left the office with a heavy heart and so many unanswered questions. Once I got into my car, to begin the long journey home, I immediately picked up my cell phone to call my mom. I suddenly remembered my mom had passed away five years prior. Nonetheless I dialed her number anyway, disconnecting the call before it rang. I began carrying on an imaginary conversation, as though my mom was on the other end of the phone. I could hear her ask in a calm manner, "What did the doctor say?" I literally responded, "I have cancer". "OH Lord Susie, we'll just have to pray and trust in the Lord." She would say.

When I got home, I told my husband, Shelby, the news. He immediately held me in his arms, I'm sure he was praying. He looked at me and said "it's going to be okay". After telling my mom and Shelby, I pondered who else I should tell. I didn't want to be the gossip of the town, you know the typical "Girl, Susie Walker has cancer!" (Most of the hometown folk refer to people using their maiden name.) I figured as the news spread false information would probably be added to it, like how much time I had to live, etc. I was very reluctant to share. In fact, I remember when I had previously heard that someone was diagnosed with cancer, I immediately thought to myself," I wonder how much time they have to live."

Little by little, day by day, I began to share the news with close friends and family. My oldest and only son Bryce, was in his first year of college. He was positive right off the bat. "Mom, cancer is not a death sentence anymore. Technology is more advanced now and people are beating it. We are warriors, you got this!" I literally felt the power in his voice and immediately believed him. When I shared with a few close friends, their response was "OH NO!" I would assure them that it was okay and that I was going to beat it. That was my initial mindset, before the treatments began.

Honestly, I never really questioned God about why I had to have cancer. I've always believed that He orders my steps and my stops, and if His will called for me to go through this, then I have no choice but to go through it. I began to reflect and think about various people I knew that had battled cancer; some lived, some were still battling and others gained their angel wings. I wondered what my verdict would be.

My husband Shelby ministered to me a lot. He would remind me of God's word. Deuteronomy 31:6 says, "Be strong and of a good courage, fear not, nor be afraid of them, for the Lord thy God, He it is that doth go with thee; He will not fail thee, nor forsake thee." God is always with us regardless of what we go through in life. He gives us the strength to endure and always sends the right people to assist us. I would often recite one of my favorite passages, Psalm 23:4 "Even though I walk through the darkest valley, I will fear no evil for you are with me; your rod and staff, they comfort me." He truly did comfort me, late at night when everyone was asleep I would talk to Him and thank Him for being with me, especially in the midst of my pain and uncertainty.

I don't know what lies ahead, none of us do. Glory to God, it's been four years that I've been in remission. The cancer is completely gone from my body. I must admit, one question plagues me and lingers in the back of my head all the time, "Will it ever come back?" I know that faith and fear don't mix, but I'm human. According to extensive research I've done, if you make it five years post cancer treatment then you're considered home free. I'm at the 3 year mark now and counting down. Every ache and pain I feel, my mind starts to wonder, "Is it back?" Thankfully it's not. I just continue to thank God for right now, another moment to get it right and be a blessing to someone else.

CHAPTER 1

SURVIVE

Write the vision, make it plain (Habakkuk 2:2)

SELF REFLECTION

1. Briefly explain an event in your life that you had absolutely no control over.

   _____
   _____
   _____
   _____
   _____

2. What are some solutions that you attempted to make things better? Did any of those options resolve the issue? Have you received your breakthrough yet?

   _____
   _____
   _____
   _____
   _____

3. Did this event change you for the better or worse? How so?

   _____
   _____
   _____
   _____
   _____
   _____
   _____
   _____

4. What scripture or quote do you gravitate to when life gets hard?

_____
_____
_____
_____
_____

5. Could you feel God's love and invisible hand at work while you were going through your valley or did you feel alone? What did HE do to let you know he was there with you?

_____
_____
_____
_____
_____

6. Choose at least 1 story, scripture or point from Chapter 1 that you could relate to. How did you relate?

_____
_____
_____
_____
_____
_____

CHAPTER 2

SUBMISSION

According to the Oxford Dictionary, submission is the action or fact of accepting or yielding to a superior force or to the will or authority of another person.

Job 22:21-23 Tells us to, "submit to God and be at peace with him; in this way prosperity will come to you. Accept instruction from his mouth and lay up his words in your heart. If you return to the Almighty, you will be restored.

LaToya's Lessons

It took me several months to come to the realization Jarrod wasn't coming back to me. Every morning (if I was lucky enough to get any sleep) I would wake up and scan our bedroom, trying to figure out if I had dreamt all of the nonsense and chaos that was taking place in my life. It didn't feel real at all. I would ask my sister, "Is this real? Did he really die?" Their words were always the same, "unfortunately yes, it's true." I would just cry. I felt so empty. My life just felt incomplete without Jarrod Jackson in it.

I knew instantly that I could not let my husband's death be in vain. There was no way that God allowed this tragedy to happen to me, without something positive coming from it. The life that was taken prematurely was worth a lot. His life was more precious than diamonds, pearls, precious gems and all the money in the world, to me.

Initially, I had many grand plans to honor Jarrod. I wanted to start a foundation and a scholarship fund. I wanted to get a highway sign with his name. I also wanted to have an annual retro dance party fundraiser because he loved to dance.

All of these things are great ideas, however, as a new widow I had absolutely no idea how the grief was going to overtake me like a ton of bricks. It stopped me dead in my tracks and all the wonderful ideas and plans I intended to follow-through with, came to a screeching halt. I had no choice but to submit.

I wasn't in control of anything during that time of my life, or at least I didn't feel like I was. God wanted me to **REST**, **REFLECT**, and **WRITE,** because once he delivered me, he was going to send me back into the wilderness to help others. Ecclesiastics 3 tells us "There is a time for everything and a season for every activity under the Heavens. A time to be born, and a time to die. A time to plant and a time to uproot. A time to kill and a time to heal. A time to tear down and a time to build. A time to weep and a time to laugh. A time to mourn and a time to dance." God had a message for me, amongst all the mess that was going on in my life, but in order for me to receive it, I had to submit, be obedient and "be still knowing that HE is God" (Psalms 46:10).

Susie's Lesson

Things were surreal for a while. I couldn't shut my mind down. I would continuously think," I have breast cancer, wow!" Slowly, but surely I adjusted to the thought of it. After the initial shock wore off, I began to get into fight mode. I began researching like crazy, trying to find out as much as I could, about this ugly disease. It wasn't enough that I had breast cancer, but I had the worst of them all, Triple Negative Breast Cancer, an ugly, aggressive type of cancer and it was growing inside of me.

After my first visit to see my surgeon things started going pretty fast, there was an immediate sense of urgency, which I appreciated. The slowest part was waiting for the results of my BRAC Gene test, which determines whether you carry an inherited BRAC mutation. It took almost two weeks and the results were not favorable. I learned that I have the gene, in addition to Triple Negative. Not only was I battling the worst type of breast cancer, but I have the BRAC Gene too. What was I supposed to do with that? It meant that I had a long road ahead. It meant that I would wonder about my fate often and that I had to purposely not think the worse. Now more than ever I had to have faith and believe that I would get through this battle. I can't emphasize enough, how important positive thinking is, it's critical!

So, how would I do it, how would I get through this? James 4:7 says, "Submit yourselves therefore to God. Resist the devil, and he will flee from you". The devil loved when I would think and dwell on negative thoughts. It wasn't easy to turn it off, because I had a lot of "what if's" running in and out of my mind. Some days were better than others, but one thing proved to be certain. Isaiah 26:3 tells us, "If we keep our minds on God then He would give us perfect peace." I often put my mind on God, his goodness, his kindness and his love. Yes, I was in a battle, but I knew I wasn't alone. I knew many others had been here too and many more would follow. I knew that there was **Purpose** for my **Pain**. I had to share my story, to encourage others to fight their battle, and stay the course regardless of the fight. Submit to God; reflect on His scriptures, keep a song of praise in your heart and mind, and you will feel His peace. A few friends including: Pastor Billy Curle, Yvonne Johnson and Cheryl "Peas" Richardson, would send me daily scriptures that really encouraged me. I appreciated the prayers, uplifting scriptures and words of encouragement it all helped me to get through and understand that submission was all I could do, I was powerless over cancer, but my Father wasn't.

CHAPTER 2

SUBMISSION

Write the vision, make it plain (Habakkuk 2:2)

SELF REFLECTION

1. This day and age when people hear the word "Submit", they associate it with weakness; even though the bible advises us to submit at different times in our lives. What does submission mean to you? Describe a time that you had to submit.

   _____
   _____
   _____
   _____
   _____
   _____
   _____

2. Why did you feel the need to submit? What was the outcome of your situation?

   _____
   _____
   _____

3. Give some examples of times submission would be the best option? Give an example of a situation you should not submit?

   _____
   _____
   _____
   _____
   _____

4. Find a scripture or quote about submission and interpret it.

_____
_____
_____
_____
_____
_____
_____
_____

5. Choose at least 1 story, scripture or point from Chapter 2 that you could relate to. How did you relate?

_____
_____
_____
_____
_____
_____
_____
_____
_____
_____
_____

CHAPTER 3

UNIQUENESS

Dictionary.com states that to be unique means, having no like or equal, unparalleled, incomparable. Existing as the only one or as the sole example single, solitary in type and characteristics.

Jeremiah 1:4-5 "The Lord gave me this message, I knew you before I formed you in your mother's womb. Before you were born I set you apart and appointed you as my prophet to the nations."

Matthew 10:31 "And the very hairs on your head are all numbered. So don't be afraid, you are more valuable to God than a whole flock of sparrows."

LaToya's Lesson

While I was in the stage of resting and reflecting, God revealed to me that I would tell my story on a national platform. I didn't know how this prophesy would come to fruition. I just knew with great certainty, that because God told me he was going to do it, He would work out all the logistics of who, where, when and how.

I remember getting a call from an Associate Producer at The Doctors TV show. It was such an exciting call to receive, to know that there was actually a possibility that they would feature my story on their show. I shared the news with an acquaintance that I was being considered to come on a show to share my story. Instead of excitement for me, I was met with; "What makes your story so unique? People lose spouses' everyday. What's so special about you?" I was literally dumbfounded, appalled, shocked and disrespected all at the same time. After only a few seconds of gathering my thoughts, my immediate response was, "because there was only 1 Jarrod and LaToya Jackson". Of course I'm aware that people lose spouses, children, parents, siblings and friends everyday. But to make a blanket statement that a loss is just another loss, without acknowledging the deceased as a unique individual, with family and friends that loved them. Personality traits, physical features, gifts and talents specifically designed for only them by our creator. All of those traits, compiled into one being, is what made him so special.

Within a two year span, two fellow "Class of 1999" classmates and I lost our husbands. Even though we all have one common denominator that connects us, losing our husbands, the circumstances in which they transitioned are all completely different. We grieve different, our lifestyles are different. The impact and imprint that each of our husband's left on this world are different and the way we choose to honor and celebrate their legacy is different. Each of our husbands were special and unique in their own way. Psalms 139:13-14 says, "You alone created my inner being. You knitted me together inside my mother. I will give thanks to you, because I have been so amazingly and miraculously made. Your works are miraculous and my soul is fully aware of this."

God loves us all because He created us in His divine image. It's our responsibility to identify what makes us unique, own our individuality, accentuate the positive and walk upright in our God-given purpose, because we all have one.

To answer my former acquaintance's question "What makes me so special?"

Because my Father who art in Heaven, says I am: and so are you!

Susie's Lesson

After my doctor told me all the ugly things about Triple Negative cancer. He had the audacity to say "Susie, it is important to be positive, being positive is KEY". Really?! He didn't exactly tell me how to do that. How exactly do I remain positive doc? You've just given me, what sounds like a death sentence. Not to mention one of the nurses told me that the doctor can tell who is going to make it, by their attitude and how they deal with it. Wow, Really? The nerve of these folks. None of them were in a fight for their lives, but they think positivity is the key to life? And they predict my outcome, by my attitude?! I wasn't sure what to make of it, but I knew one thing, regardless of how I was feeling, I was determined that they would see me in a positive light. They would know each and every time they saw me, that I was giving it all I had. I used my creativity and came up with a unique way to show just how "positive" I was and in the process hype myself up.

I ordered pink boxing gloves and wore them to treatment every week. Our local news channel featured a story around this unique concept of me wearing pink boxing gloves to chemo treatments. I remember the first time my doctor saw them, he had a big smile on his face. I was certain that He believed in me and knew that not only did I come to FIGHT, but I intended to WIN!

Late in the midnight hour, while my family was sleeping, I would put the gloves on and hype myself up. I was physically weak, but mentally strong. I would do a lot of self-talk and tell myself that I can and will get through these chemo treatments. One day, I would be physically strong again and able to do activities with my family. I told myself that I would go to work and grind with or without hair. Even though I had long thick hair, I would, always wear wigs. Chemo treatments made my head hot and it was nearly impossible to continue wearing wigs. My God-sister, Fay, made a really cute wig for me and I wore it to work, but after a couple of hours I yanked it off. I decided I would walk out of my office and down the hallway rocking my bald head. My co-workers smiled and complimented my new look, the students gave me kudos too, after that day it was the new me.

I rocked the bald with confidence. People said I had the right head for it, whatever that means. Even if I didn't, I was going to rock it anyway! I got tired of worrying about how people would receive my new look. What would they say about me? I've always had hair and this was new territory for me. The hotter I became, the more uncomfortable I was in that hot wig. In that moment, I realized that I had to be me. Perfect in God's sight, with or without hair. It was so empowering to accept myself, flaws and all.

I am different, I am unique, but in God's eyes, I'm perfect!

CHAPTER 3

UNIQUENESS

Write the vision, make it plain (Habakkuk 2:2)

SELF REFLECTION

1. God loves us so much, he designed us all completely different from one another. No one in the world has the exact same DNA or fingerprint as you. Do you realize you are special in the eyes of God? What are characteristics that make you unique?

   _____
   _____
   _____
   _____
   _____
   _____
   _____

2. What are some gifts and talents that God has blessed you with? Are you using those gifts to honor and glorify God? If not, why?

   _____
   _____
   _____
   _____
   _____
   _____
   _____

3. Are there any characteristics that make you unique that you don't like? Why don't you embrace it?

___

4. What scripture or quote do you gravitate to regarding loving the person God created you to be?

___

5. Choose at least 1 story, scripture or point from Chapter 3 that you could relate to. How did you relate?

___

CHAPTER 4

RESTORATION

According to Dictionary.com, *restoration* is restitution of something taken away or lost. A return of something to a former, original, normal, or unimpaired condition. The act of restoring, renewal, revival or re-establishment.

Deuteronomy 30:3 says, "God, your God, will restore everything you lost; he'll have compassion on you; he'll come back and pick up the pieces from all the places where you were scattered."

LaToya's Lesson

The woman "formerly known" as LaToya Calbert is dead, cremated and scattered across the world, never to be put back together or made whole again. I died a very slow, painful death. One riddled with longsuffering, grief, emptiness, pain, loneliness, and confusion.

Everything that has transpired in my life from 12/17/14, to this very moment has been unbelievable, mind-blowing and life changing. Once I began going in-ward and seeking God, instead of outwardly looking to people to pacify, rectify and heal me, His muffled voice that had always been there, became clearer and more apparent than ever before. Just like a radio with annoying interference and static, you can make out some of the words, you know the song is playing you just can't hear it clearly; but when you get closer to the source, when you get out of the woods, out of the desert, you can begin to hear clearly, you can hear all of the words, the melody, the instrumentation, the bass line. It all became clearer, when I began to draw nearer to my Father.

As I began to plead to God for HELP, in my most vulnerable state, I asked him "why me"? He responded with "WHY NOT YOU"? In that moment I realized the person formerly known as LaToya Calbert was not exempt from life, hurt, pain, and tragedy. I also learned during my time in the valley, while praying and seeking God that HE knew I would not sit in my pain, he knew I would take it and use it to help someone else. He told me to write my story and that in time, He would give me a platform to share my story to help others who are also in the valley, fighting to break free.

I will never be LaToya Calbert again. The girl who went through her first 33 years, looking at life through rose colored glasses. The old me was gone, but God promised to revive me and not only restore me, but to make me BETTER than I was before. This new girl, this transformed woman, Mrs. LaToya Jackson is better, kinder, more loving, empathetic, relatable and most importantly authentic. Everyone does not allow the heartache, tragedy, loss and pain they've endured to help them grow into who they were meant to be. As ironic as it may sound, everything we go through in life is a part of the pruning process to help us become our highest self. The highs and lows of life are all meant to help us grow. When we open our minds and realize that we are vessels sent here to do the work of the most high, God can begin to mold us into who we were ultimately created to be, but it's our choice. Romans 12:2 reminds us, "Do not conform to the pattern of this world, but be transformed by the renewing of your mind, that by testing, you may discern what is the will of God, what is good, pleasing and perfect in his sight."

Susie's Lesson

My husband, Shelby and I have been married 20 years in April. I can't believe it has been that long. Before the cancer battle, we were on the brink of divorce. Shelby and I are totally opposites; he's calm and laid back, takes his time doing everything, including answering my questions. Me on the other hand, I am spontaneous, always rushing and constantly on the go. Our extreme opposite characters often clashed, because we were just so different. The one thing we had in common was our faith in God and love for our family. Other than that, I felt that I had out grown him, he just couldn't keep up with me. However, while I was battling cancer, Shelby was with me and beside me EVERY step of the way. I recall him holding me when I first told him the diagnosis. He held me tight and assured me that it would be alright. I recall seeing him numerous times on his knees praying and petitioning Heaven on my behalf. He kept the family afloat, running errands, taking the kids to school & activities, he cooked, cleaned, and went to all my appointments, ALWAYS pronto while NEVER complaining. He kept me encouraged; my protector, my rock, my hero.

Needless to say, after it was all said and done, the love was rekindled; two opposites attract all over again and our marriage has been restored.

CHAPTER 4

RESTORATION

Write the vision, make it plain (Habakkuk 2:2)

SELF REFLECTION

1. Briefly explain a time in your life that something or someone was taken from you.

   _____
   _____
   _____

2. Was the change in your best interest?

   _____
   _____
   _____

3. Did this event change you for the better or worse? How so?

   _____
   _____
   _____

4. Did God replace what you lost with something better?

   _____
   _____

5. Describe a time that you felt God restoring your life or changing you for the better?

   _____
   _____
   _____

CHAPTER 5

VESSEL

According to Merriam Webster, a *vessel* is a person into whom some quality (such as grace) is infused."

2 Timothy 2:21 says, "Therefore, if anyone cleanses himself from these things, he will be a vessel for honor, sanctified, useful to the Master, prepared for every good work."

LaToya's Lesson

In the last chapter on "Restoration", I talked about being a vessel for God. When I accepted the fact that I wasn't just put here to roam aimlessly, doing what I wanted, when I wanted; but realizing my life has meaning far beyond my imagination and that my purpose depends on my acceptance and obedience. I willingly accepted the call and pleaded to God to use me, anyway He sees fit.

After the loss of my husband, my family and I (8 of us) were all crammed into 1 small bedroom; 2 beds, 1 air mattress and 1 bathroom at the Fairfield Marriott for 3 whole days. They covered me and tightly swaddled me with their unconditional love, unity and support. I thank God for them! During that time, because we were in such closed quarters, I would go into the hallway of the hotel, to get a second to think and be alone. One night while in the hallway, one of the managers kept roaming the hallways doing his nightly routine. It was 3 times he passed me, I originally thought he was keeping an eye on me and I was offended. On his 3rd time passing me, he noticed me crying and he finally asked me if I was okay. I shared with him that I had just lost my husband. I didn't know what to do and I was devastated. This perfect stranger hugged me so tightly, with compassion and sincerity. He listened to me and then he began to speak. He shared with me, he also was once in my position. A year after he was married, the love of his life was diagnosed with cancer and died. I knew instantly he was sent as a vessel from God to console me and share his story with me. He went on to tell me about how his life spiralled out of control, he began drinking to numb the pain. He remarried to a woman he knew was not the one, but he admitted he was seeking the love he had with his first wife. For years he struggled with substance abuse and toxic relationships.

Finally his wife came to him in a dream and shared with him that she was ok. She wanted him to be happy and let go. He stopped drinking, divorced his abusive wife and chose to actively seek happiness. After years of mourning, he found another woman that he grew to love just as much as his first wife and they built a family together and are madly in love. He told me, "I know right now it feels like the end of the world, but you will be ok." Just thinking about that moment brings me to tears because I knew it was a God moment. God orchestrated everything about our chance meeting, in the hallway of the Beachwood, Fairfield Inn on Dec 19, 2014 around 11pm. I hung on to that man's words "it's gonna be ok". Even when I really didn't believe it would be ok, I told myself it would. If God could bring him out and allow him to be a VESSEL for me, then surely at some point, God would also use me as a vessel to help someone else going through a valley of uncertainty. I prayed that God would turn things around for me, as well, and that in due season, I would share my story of tragedy and triumph to a lost soul and offer a sincere hug and a kind word of encouragement, reassuring them that they, too, "will be ok".

Susie's Lesson

In the Bible, a vessel signifies a person that God specifically chose and used for a purpose. Jesus said that Paul was a chosen vessel in Acts 9:15 (KJV) **[15] But the Lord said unto him, Go thy way: for he is a chosen vessel unto me, to bear my name before the Gentiles, and kings, and the children of Israel.**

Life is not always a bed of roses, we all have a bitter cup that we must drink from at some point. Whether it's due to the: loss of a job, sickness, divorce, or death. At some point, everyone will have to drink from a bitter cup, unless their life is unfortunately cut short. It's about us enduring and getting through it and then sharing our experiences and testimonies to help others do the same.

A former classmate contacted me via Facebook and said she needed to speak with me. I gave her my phone number and told her to call anytime, she never called. However, I ran into her at Walmart, as we both were grocery shopping. It was then that she informed me she had been diagnosed with breast cancer. I shared a little about my journey on my page and she wanted to connect with me and get more feedback about my experiences while fighting the disease. I informed her that I had the worst out of 30 different types of breast cancer, Triple Negative. However, fortunately for me, it was caught during stage 1. I don't recall the exact stage she was in, but it wasn't the 4th stage, which is the final stage of the disease.

As I shared my story I could tell she felt a sense of hope. I offered to pray with her and she accepted. We held hands and prayed, right there in the middle of an aisle at Walmart. We didn't talk much afterwards, but I followed her on Facebook and watched as she shared her journey.

Unfortunately, due to complications from a procedure, she required long term care and was moved into a nursing home; never to return to her home again. Eventually, she transitioned and gained her Angel wings.

I can't begin to express how terrible I felt about it, I harbored a sense of guilt, because "I'm still here and she's not". Although we were fighting different types of cancer, we both had a battle and unfortunately she experienced complications.

I know people who are extremely private and would never disclose their personal struggles and victories, while enduring such a horrific disease. However, others (such as myself) don't mind sharing our cancer battle. I believe that we go through things, so that we can help others understand they aren't alone. We are vessels allowing God to use us to change the direction of someone else's life by giving them hope.

CHAPTER 5

VESSEL

Write the vision, make it plain (Habakkuk 2:2)

SELF REFLECTION

1. Explain a time that God put someone in your life to comfort you, do you feel they were being used by God or do you believe it was luck?

   _____
   _____
   _____

2. Explain a time you were used as a vessel to help someone else?

   _____
   _____
   _____

3. How did these events impact you and your faith?

   _____
   _____
   _____

4. Could you feel God's love and invisible hand at work while you were going through your valley or did you feel alone? What did HE do to let you know he was there with you?

   _____
   _____
   _____
   _____

CHAPTER 6

IMAGINE

According to Collin's Dictionary, *imagine* is to make a mental image of; form an idea or <u>notion</u> of; <u>conceive</u> in the mind; create by the imagination.

1 Cor 2:9 But, as it is written, "What no eye has seen, nor ear heard, nor the heart of man imagined, what God has prepared for those who love him"

LaToya's Lesson

Throughout life as a child and even as an adult I've always had a very vivid imagination. I would envision what I wanted to happen in my life; the car, the man, the ability to travel and so forth and eventually those things would manifest. The mind/brain is the most powerful organ in our body. Once I realized that I could really will, whatever I wanted, simply by thinking it, believing it and making the necessary strides to unleash it, I became a visionary.

I momentarily lost my ability to imagine, when Jarrod died. I could not see anything passed the season I was in. In my mind, although Jarrod was literally absent from his earthly shell, it was completely opposite for me. I was present in the physical (my earthly shell), but on the inside I was a hollow soul. I hated everything about living and the only thing I could envision was my death.

Thank God for intercessors! I know people all over the world were praying for little ole' me. Slowly but surely, my mind began to clear just enough for me to hear a word from God. "Your life is not your own LaToya, it belongs to me. I'm going to give you a platform to share your story to help others." I heard Him loud and clear. There was a lot of clutter, chaos, and confusion in my life at that time. People that I thought would be there for me, were nowhere to be found. My mom and dad were dealing with sickness and personal demons. I was battling with a chronic pain condition, my husband's family, and my previous employer regarding a discrimination case. How much could one person take? All it took was to hear the voice of the Almighty, reassuring me that there is indeed a mighty MESSAGE from all of the MESS, taking place in my life. That one seed planted gave me hope that life would get easier. I began to write, envisioning myself sharing my book with the world. Helping others also going through the struggles of life.

Thank God I got my mind back. I got my ambition back. I got my zeal for life back. Lastly, I got my vivid imagination back, all from one seed. I've grown leaps and bounds spiritually, and now realize EVERYTHING I was enduring in that moment and for the rest of my days has divine purpose.

Susie's Lesson

Habakkuk 2:2 tells us to write the vision and make it plan…

I am a creative person, a big dreamer! Like Martin Luther King Jr., I have a vision that I will share my story with the world and give a sense of hope to others that are fighting the cancer battle. I have a vision that I will encourage, educate and empower others to be an advocate for themselves, their health, or the health of a loved one. Technology and the world of medicine are ever evolving. I continue to research advancements and holistic approaches to the treatment of cancer, and preventative measures, to share with others, so that they can make informed decisions about their treatment and overall health.

I have a vision that one day, I will be able to allow someone who is going through the cancer battle to live in my current home; without worrying about paying rent and being financially overwhelmed about having a roof over their head, while fighting for their life.

I have a vision that one day I will be a much healthier me; eating right with adequate weight loss and gaining mental clarity.

I have a vision that I will be in a season of overflow regarding my emotional, spiritual and financial breakthrough.

CHAPTER 6

IMAGINE

Write the vision, make it plain (Habakkuk 2:2)

SELF REFLECTION

1. Briefly explain a time in your life when you used imagery to get you through a tough time.

   _____
   _____
   _____

2. What are some goals/dreams/aspirations that you've been able to manifest, that started out in your imagination?

   _____
   _____
   _____

3. What thoughts and actions helped to bring your dreams to reality?

   _____
   _____
   _____
   _____

4. What dreams do you currently have that seem to be a figment of your imagination? How do you plan to make them a reality?

   _____
   _____
   _____

CHAPTER 7

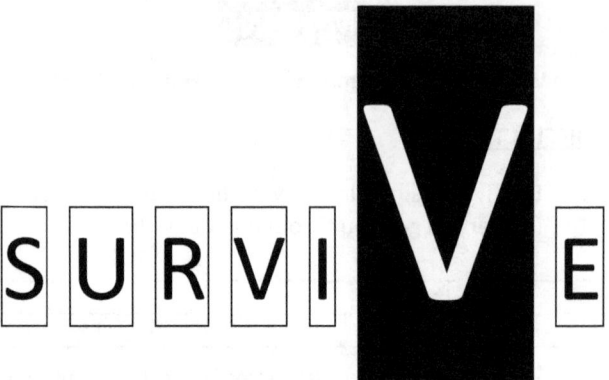

VICTORY

Merriam Webster states, *victory* is to overcome an enemy or antagonist, achievement of mastery or success in a struggle or endeavor against odds or difficulties.

Deuteronomy 20:4 "For the LORD your God is the one who goes with you to fight for you against your enemies to give you victory."

LaToya's Lesson

God is undefeated! I think, at times, when life tries to weigh us down, we tend to forget that. I can't count how many times God has made a way, out of no way for me and my family.

I remember getting unexpected checks in the mail when I needed them most. I remember my mother being so sick and on her death bed, when GOD came in and healed her body. I remember travelling alone all over the country roughly 300 days out of the year, for almost 4 years, mainly driving from as far east as Boston, MA to as far west as Los Angeles, CA and never had a fender bender or any type of issues. All due to God's unwavering love and protection over me.

But why is it at times when life begins to throw darts at us, that we begin to panic? It's almost as if we've forgotten that quickly of God's track record of success. I believe its human nature, especially when we hit an all-time low and circumstances are unfamiliar to anything we've ever experienced, we forget just how powerful God is. The word says God is so powerful that he "created

EVERYTHING on Heaven, Earth and the sea in six days and on the 7th day HE rested" (Genesis 1:1). That's a bad man!

It took me a little while, but I finally realized that the only way I would get any relief from the hopelessness I felt, was by allowing God to fight this battle and every other battle for me. The load was way too heavy for me, so either HE would handle it or it would fester. Losing a spouse, dealing with a sick parent, fighting a corporation about inequality and so many other things simultaneously, were all outside of my expertise.

Only a crazy, totally insane person, with absolutely no experience in boxing, would get into the ring with Floyd "Money" Mayweather. The man is undefeated! So why would I attempt to fight death, grief, sickness, envy, discrimination and so on, by myself? At one point in my life, I may have tried to fix it all, but not now. I realize that God specializes in victories and because I'm HIS daughter, a royal heir to the highest throne, my daddy, way-maker, mind elevator, heart-fixer, Elohim, and Elshaddai, will fight and WIN the battle for me and he'll do the same for you.

Susie's Lesson

One of my favorite songs says, "Victory is mine, victory is mine, victory today is mine." I am so glad to be here living my life, not a mundane life, but a life of purpose.

I have the victory of seeing my first born, Bryce, graduate Cum Laude from the University of Kentucky. I have the victory of seeing my middle child, Brooke, attend high school and work her very first job. I have the victory of watching my baby girl, Bria, attend middle school and make the cheerleading squad, also becoming a team captain.

With a heart of praise and gratitude, I'm singing "Victory is mine, victory is mine, victory TODAY is mine. I told Satan to get thee behind, Victory today is MINE!" My husband Shelby and I, will soon celebrate another wedding anniversary and because of what we've been through, we have a greater appreciation for one another and for life.

I declare and decree, that I will watch my children grow into successful adults. I will also watch their children grow into successful adults. I speak dominion over sickness and disease, binding cancer and every other stronghold that attempts to attack me. I send it back to the pits of hell from whence it came.

I declare and decree that my marriage, my family, and friendships will continue to be solid, healthy and fruitful. Shelby and I will travel, enjoy life together, and strive to be a blessing to all those we encounter.

"Victory today is mine."

CHAPTER 7

VICTORY

Write the vision, make it plain (Habakkuk 2:2)

SELF REFLECTION

1. Reflect on a time in your life that you felt powerless. How did God intervene and give you the victory over that situation?

_____
_____
_____
_____
_____
_____
_____
_____

2. How did you thank God for giving you the victory?

_____
_____
_____
_____
_____
_____
_____

CHAPTER 8

EXPECTANCY

According to Definition.com, *expectancy* is anticipatory belief or desire. The feeling of hope that something exciting, interesting, or good is about to happen.

Jeremiah 29:11 "For I know the thoughts that I think toward you, saith the LORD, thoughts of peace, and not of evil, to give you an expected end."

Stand On God's Promises

In closing, God has given us free will to make decisions regarding our own lives and which paths we feel are best for us. Often times our decisions are based on our individual life circumstances and the cards that we have been dealt.

Many crisis that arise in our lives are completely out of our control. Susie and I, didn't ask to have our lives ravished by death and disease. However, God decided to add each of those chapters to "The Book of Susie" and "The Book of LaToya". Thankfully, we both realized that those extremely painful chapters in our lives were just that, a chapter, not the entire book. Through our individual struggles, we realize that nothing in this life is coincidental.

Although our stories are completely opposite, fight or flight mode naturally kicks in when life gets tough and throws grenades that could kill, steal and destroy. We both chose to not only FIGHT, but to return to the battlefield to help usher others to safety who are running for their lives. No matter the dilemma, the steps taken to SURVIVE and ultimately THRIVE remain the same:

- **Submit** to God and realize that HE has created us all in His image and that we are all special and **unique** in His sight.
- After the struggles of life have torn us down, God wants to rebuild and **restore** everything we thought we lost and use us as individual **vessels** to spread the good news of HIS abundant love for us.
- All we have to do is humbly come to him and ask for what we want, **imagining** better days.
- Truly believing that God will deliver on HIS promises and that whatever you're going through, you will be **victorious.**
- Lastly, **expect** the overflow! When you ask, be ready for HIM to put the people and resources in place to help elevate you.

Life can be hard at times, but we have a God that will carry us through, if we allow HIM. He not only wants us to survive, but HE wants us to **THRIVE.** John 10:10 says "I come so they may have life, and that they might have it more abundantly." Stand on HIS word and watch the PAIN turn to PURPOSE.

WALK IN IT!

CHAPTER 8

EXPECTANCY

Write the vision, make it plain (Habakkuk 2:2)

SELF REFLECTION

1. When God blesses you with the overflow and the breakthrough what will you do with it? How will this change your life? How will you glorify God for HIS goodness?

___

CHAPTER 9

AFTER THE
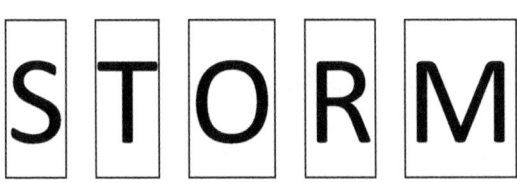

When the storms of life come, the wicked are whirled away, but the Godly have a lasting foundation. *(Proverbs 10:25)*

To be honest, we both have our days that the tribulations of life attempt to steal our joy and take us back to those people, places and things that God has already delivered us from. We are human and the flesh is weak, but God's word is true. His word says that the storms will come, but HE has already given us dominion over them. It's up to us, to go backwards into disparity or move forward into deliverance.

LaToya's Lesson

I go back and forth; some days I have an "I can do all things through Christ" mentality, other days I crawl into a ball and cry myself to sleep from sorrow. However, I don't stay there!!!

The words of Pastor Donnie Mclurkin ring true:

"Get back up again

Get back up again

Get back up again

For a saint, is just a sinner

Who fell down, and got up"

Honestly, I've been through much more than just losing my husband since his passing in 2014. When I really reflect on everything, I admire myself. I admire myself that I'm not in a mental institution. I realize that a lot of others have ended their own lives, for a lot less. I attribute all of my resilience to my faith. I'm grateful for a praying mother and father that instilled the love of God in me at an early age, otherwise I firmly believe I would be an alcoholic, drug addicted or maybe even dead. I've tried to drink myself into a drunken stupor, because I didn't want to feel, but God wouldn't let me! I've attempted to force relationships with men, which I knew God didn't create for me, but God wouldn't let me settle!

I'm learning to love myself and truly be okay with being alone. I'm complete with just me, myself, and I.

My next soulmate, will be my complement!

Susie's Lesson

A cancer diagnosis may be a part of my life, but it does not define my life. As a social worker, I have always been an advocate for others, helping to give them a voice. Now I am advocating, to raise awareness about breast cancer.

Yes, because of breast cancer I loss some things; my hair, breast, and reproductive organs, to name a few.

However, I gained several gifts of greater value; the gift of forgiveness, thankfulness, faith and appreciation for life, I didn't realize I lacked.

Since we are being totally honest, I live with daily uncertainty. The thought of a reoccurrence enters my mind often. There was a time that it consumed me just thinking about "what if it comes back?" It seems like everywhere I turn, I hear stories that someone's cancer came back with a vengeance and before you know it they're gone!

One day I was in a boutique looking for a statement necklace. While shopping, simply minding my own business, I overheard the store clerk and a customer talking about their mutual friend. They were going back and forth and I couldn't help but to listen in. They were talking so loud that I could not ignore them if I wanted to.

"I can't believe Mary's cancer came back, we thought she had beaten it" they stated. They went on to say that she passed away, from the most deadly, vengeful, dreaded type, *triple negative;* the one I had.

I was upset at how they were discussing the matter as though no one else was around. They had no clue the torment I felt in that moment. When the customer finally left, I took my purchase to the clerk and politely told her that I overheard their conversation and was deeply affected by it. "I too had triple negative breast cancer" I stated. She apologized and said "bless you". "Bless me" I thought. "Really lady!"

After getting into my car, I called LaToya as I sobbed and told her what happened. I told her how much I appreciate our friendship and the fact that God brought us together. I proceeded to tell her what I wanted her to do regarding my family, when my journey ends. She allowed me to talk and get it out, but she reminded me that someone else's story is not my story.

As I began to reflect on my life and this tedious journey, I became overwhelmed with gratitude. Instead of sadness, I switched my thinking to making the most of my life, by loving more and sharing with others.

I spoke with another survivor and I asked her how she copes with fear of reoccurrence. She simply stated by enjoying each day given. None of us will live forever.

When you appreciate the life you've been blessed with EVERYDAY, whenever God is ready to call us home we'll be ready.

So I've vowed to get so busy really living, that I don't have time to fear the inevitable. LaToya also reminded me that because of my research and educating myself, I have the tools that I need to move forward and be proactive to do everything in my power to prevent a reoccurrence and she was right. I have learned so much about this disease and now is the time to act on it!

Accountability Continues

We have both vowed to help inspire one another and hold one another accountable, when we may be slipping on our goals, positive self-talk and even faith. That's why sisterhood, friendship and fellowship with other believers and likeminded individuals is so important.

LaToya's purpose is to inspire, encourage, empower and help infuse God's love everywhere she goes. People are hurting and everyone is going through something. People from all walks of life, can benefit from a word of inspiration from someone who has been through Hell and back, but is still standing.

Susie's purpose is to help spread awareness, because everyone is affected by cancer in one way or another; whether it is you, someone you know or a friend of a friend. According to the **Breast Cancer Research Foundation** "every two minutes a woman is diagnosed with breast cancer". **The American Cancer Society** states that "the rate of cancer diagnoses is slightly increasing by 0.3% per year in African American women compared to women of other races and ethnicities. I believe that one factor is the prevalence of obesity in the black community, which is something I have too struggled with, for most of my life. I am trying really hard to change my relationship with food. It's a matter of reconditioning my mind and body as I attempt to start a new regimen, to help preserve my life.

Many warriors are relieved and excited to be done with breast cancer treatment, but on another note, many of us worry and live in fear of it coming back. Always remember **"knowledge is power!"** Educate yourself and research for yourself. There are also many holistic approaches you can take as preventative measures. We need to be proactive instead of reactive, to totally annihilate this demon! I encourage you to live your life with purpose and passion every single day.

Let's Stay Connected

Susie is involved in many organizations that help provide resources to cancer patients and survivors. The two she holds closest to her heart are ***Susie's Strength***, which is an initiative she founded after experiencing first-hand the financial strain cancer added to an already difficult situation. She has also teamed up with an organization called ***Jill's Wish*** that provides financial resources to cancer patients. Susie received assistance from *Jill's Wish* at one point in time and is now partnering with them, to pay it forward, while also serving on their board.

Join Susie as she launches her first weight-loss challenge. Your participation is welcomed and encouraged. It will be a fun, friendly meeting place for people from all over, to unite, inspire and encourage one another to take back their health. Find out more at:

Website: susiesstrength.com

Facebook: Susie Walker-Byrd

Instagram: susiesstrength

LaToya has written numerous books that include:

365 Days of Separation: A memoir/ Christian living novel about the first year after losing her new husband and the struggles she faced.

Unfair Encounters: A book about the supernatural occurrence's LaToya endured, the first few years after losing her husband Jarrod, and the different ways he communicated with her, from the other side.

I Make Pain Look Pretty: A book about challenges that continue to arise after moving on after loss, the difficulties in dating this millennium as a widow, family and friend drama and much more.

God Loves Chocolate: Is a children's book about loving the skin you're in and self-acceptance, as a young black boy.

God Loves Chocolate Girls: Is the girl's version of God Love's Chocolate. It tackles the topic of colorism, but on a child's level.

My Name Is Zari: Is a children's book about a little girl that is unapologetically happy with the qualities that make her who she is.

To stay informed of book release dates, speaking engagements and all things LaToya, you can check her out at:

Website: latoyatjackson.com

Blog: latoyatjackson.wordpress.com

Facebook: mrslatoyatjackson

Instagram: latoya_t_jackson

Be Blessed

Meet The Authors

LaToya T. Jackson, is a visionary, who believes with God all things are possible. Holding a Bachelors in Management and Marketing, she has worked in project coordination & management, but has also owned several small businesses. From an early age, writing has been a form of expression & therapy for LaToya. Her **PURPOSE** is helping others, her **PASSION** is traveling the world.

Susie Walker-Byrd, is passionate about helping others, obtaining her Master's Degree in Social Work; working tirelessly for over 20 years to enhance the lives of others. Married to her "BFF and Boaz" Shelby, for 20+ years. Susie is also a mother of 1 son (Bryce), and 2 daughters (Brooke & Bria). Susie loves spending time with family & all things Oprah.

www.ingramcontent.com/pod-product-compliance
Lightning Source LLC
LaVergne TN
LVHW051150080426
835508LV00021B/2565